Kwanzaa in Hawai`i

Dr. Ayin M. Adams

Pacific Raven Press Publishing, Hawai`i

Copyright© Ayin M. Adams, Ph.D.

ISBN-13
978-0984212287-5
ISBN-10
09841228-7-7

First Edition: March 2012

Cover Design and Illustrations by Stacy Comer
Typesetting by Saforabu Graphix
Dr. Kathryn Waddell Takara photo taken by Gary Dymally
Kwanzaa Photos Copyright© Ayin M. Adams, Ph.D.

Published by PACIFIC RAVEN PRESS
P.O. Box 678, Ka`a`awa, HI 96730 USA
www.pacificravenpress.com
Email: pacificravenpress@gmail.com
Telephone : 1-808-276-6864 USA
Fax Number: 1-808-237-8974 USA

Published in the United States of America.

No part of this book may be reproduced or transmitted in any form or by any means, electronic, mechanical, photocopying, or otherwise, without the express written consent of Ayin M. Adams, Ph.D. and Pacific Raven Press Publishing.

Printed in USA.

Also by Dr. Ayin M. Adams

For Ladies Only: Dedicated to the Color Pink
African Americans in Hawai`i: A Search for Identity
The Woods Deep Inside Me
Walking Through My Fire
Walking In Sappho's Garden

Table of Contents

Introduction	vi
What is Kwanzaa	1
Nguzo Saba (The Seven Principles)	2
Traditional Symbols of Kwanzaa	3
Harambee Chant	5
Yam Festival	6
Recipes for Kwanzaa	7
Poems for Kwanzaa	13
Umoja	14
Kujichagulia / Unmask Us Now	16
Ujima / I Lit a Candle For you Today	18
Ujamaa / Heritage (Hawai`i)	20
Nia	21
Kuumba / My Link to Mother	22
Imani Is	24
Community Photos	27
Locations of Photos	30
Additional Credits	30

Introduction

Kwanzaa is a celebratory period of seven days from December 26 - January 1 that acknowledges spirit, the ancestors, and seven principles for living more harmoniously in a ritual that is popular with many African Americans. It celebrates certain values to be embraced by the community, the family, and the individual to help create better, more productive, and fulfilled lives. Although the African American community is small in the Hawaiian Islands, resident groups of African Americans and their friends and families gather together in a tradition to celebrate the 7 principles of Kwanzaa at the end of each year. The principles are: umoja, ujima, ujamaa, kujuchagulia, nia, kuumba, and imani. Dr. Ayin M. Adams has put together this delightfully creative and informative book to share the philosophical values, cultural poetry, recipes, and photographs of the unique beauty of the Hawaiian Islands and enhance the meaning, scope, depth, and intimate ritual of Kwanzaa.

Kwanzaa in Hawai`i is beautifully designed using textures that symbolize the natural state of African culture with the use of woods, woven mats, and paper textures. African Masks are worn in rituals and reserved for special occasions, including harvests. The illustrations in the book symbolize traditional African art, rituals, and celebration, including two symbols for the Sun Gods. The disk-headed Akuaba figure on page iii symbolizes good luck. Originally, the Akuaba were carried by women who hoped to conceive a child. On page 8, the Cihongo Mask from the Tschokwe People (Zaire and Angola) is seen as a symbol of wealth and power, and it is used during the initiation and circumcision rites of young boys. On page 10, the African Fang Masks from Gabon were worn by spiritual leaders to ward off evil spirits, or as a symbol of wealth and prosperity.

Kwanzaa in Hawai`i is a wonderful book for children and adults, for people of all races and cultures, genders and abilities, to encourage the conscious instillation of values to live by in order to strengthen one's personal and collective lives. A unique presentation!

Kathryn Waddell Takara, Ph.D., author of *Frank Marshall Davis: The Fire and the Phoenix (A Critical Biography)*

Kwanzaa

Kwanzaa is an African American holiday which celebrates family, community and culture. It is celebrated during a special time of the year from December 26th through January 1st .

Kwanzaa is a Swahili word which means first fruits. It is a celebration of the harvest. It is a time when people join together and share the first fruits, dance and drum and honor the ancestors.

Nguzo Saba
(The Seven Principles)

 **Umoja** (oo-MOH-jah) Unity
To strive for and maintain unity in the family, community, nation and race.

 **Kujichagulia** (koo-gee-CHAH-goo-lee-ah) Self-Determination
To define ourselves, name ourselves, create for ourselves and speak for ourselves.

 Ujima (OO-GEE-mah) Collective Work and Responsibility
To build and maintain our community together and make our brother's and sister's problems our problems and to solve them together.

 **Ujamaa** (oo-jah-MAH-ah) Cooperative Economics
To build and maintain our own stores, shops and other businesses and to profit from them together.

 **Nia** (NEE-ah) Purpose
To make our collective vocation the building and developing of our community in order to restore our people to their traditional greatness.

 **Kuumba** (Koo-OOM-0bah) Creativity
To do always as much as we can, in the way we can, in order to leave our community more beautiful and beneficial than we inherited it.

 Imani (ee-MAH-nee) Faith
To believe with all our heart in our people, our parents, our teachers, our leaders and the righteousness and victory of our struggle.

Traditional Symbols of Kwanzaa

Kwanzaa has seven basic symbols and two supplemental ones. Each represents values and concepts reflective of African culture and contributive to community building and reinforcement. The basic symbols in Swahili and then in English are:

Mazao (The Crops)
These are symbolic of African harvest celebrations and of the rewards of productive and collective labor.

Mkeka (The Mat)
This is symbolic of our tradition and history and therefore, the foundation on which we build.

Kinara (The Candle Holder)
This is symbolic of our roots, our parent people—Continental Africans.

Muhindi (The Corn)
This is symbolic of our children and our future which they embody. It symbolizes growth.

Mishumaa Saba (The Seven Candles)
These are symbolic of the Nguzo Saba, the Seven Principles, a set of values which African people are urged to live by in order to rescue and reconstruct their lives in their own image and according to their own needs.

Kikombe cha Umoja (The Unity Cup)
This is symbolic of the foundational principle and practice of unity. It is used to toast and honor the ancestors.

Zawadi (The Gifts)
These are symbolic of the labor and love of parents and the commitments made and kept by the children. They are gifts of love for the children.

The two supplemental symbols are:

Bendera (The Flag)
The colors of the Kwanzaa flag are black, red and green; black for the people, red for their struggle, and green for the future.

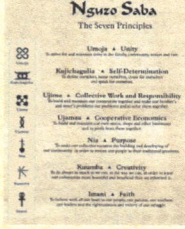
Nguzo Saba Poster (Poster of The Seven Principles)

Harambee Chant

Harambee (hah-RAHM-beh) is a Swahili word which means, let us join together. Kwanzaa should be celebrated in the spirit of harambee.

Ha-ha-ha-a-rambee

Ha-a-ram-bee

Let us join together now

Let's join together now!

Use hand clapping and drum to accompany chant.

Yam Festival

The yam festival marks the end of an abundant food-producing harvest. African people have always had festivals at the time of the harvest. In Ghana the Yam Festival (Homowo) lasts three days. The festival begins with a cleansing ceremony to honor family members who have died. Farmers give thanks to the gods who ensure a good harvest. Twins and triplets are honored during this time as a special gift from God.

A yam is large root vegetable that looks like a tube. People often confuse a yam with a sweet potato. Yams come from Africa while sweet potatoes are from Asia. Yams can be stored for 2 months in dark and cool areas. They can also be dried and turned into flour for longer storage. Yams are associated with Thanksgiving in the United States. When you have yams at your Thanksgiving dinner, think about the villagers in Ghana and Nigeria, they too are giving thanks, especially for this special food

Yams are an important crop in Ghana. During Homowo, they are taken from the ground and are carried to the village. Then they are blessed by the chief. Special foods made from yams are served. Mashed yams with hard boiled eggs are an important part of the festival.

During Homowo people wear a kind of toga made from Kente cloth which is brightly colored. The festival ends with a big feast. People dance and sing to the sounds of drums. When a child is born into the society of Ghana, a meal of yam and other ingredients is prepared for relatives and the midwife who delivers the baby.

RECIPES FOR KWANZAA

Yam Potato Pie

Ingredients
2 medium size yams
½ cup butter or margarine
½ cup sugar
1 tablespoon nutmeg
2 tablespoons cinnamon
2 eggs
1/8 teaspoon salt
¼ teaspoon lemon flavor
¼ cup coconut, ½ cup walnuts
1 ½ cup milk

Directions
Boil yams in skin until tender. Cool. Remove skin and place pulp in a large mixing bowl. Add eggs, milk, sugar and butter. Beat with electric or hand mixer. Add salt, lemon, nutmeg, cinnamon, walnuts and coconut. Pour into unbaked pie shell. Bake at 350 degrees for 40 minutes.

African Squash & Yams

Ingredients
1 small Onion; chopped, pared & cut into 1" pieces
2 tablespoon Oil
1 cup coconut Milk
1 lb Hubbard squash; pared and cut into 1 inch pieces
1/2 teaspoon salt
1/2 teaspoon ground cinnamon
2 medium size Yams or sweet potatoes
1/4 teaspoon ground cloves

Directions
Cook and stir onion in oil in 10-inch skillet over medium heat until tender. Stir in remaining ingredients. Bring to boil, reduce heat, cover and simmer 10 minutes. Simmer, uncovered, stirring occasionally, until vegetables are tender, about 5 minutes longer.

African Green Pepper & Spinach

Ingredients
1 medium onion; chopped
1 medium green pepper; chopped
1 tablespoon oil
1 medium tomato; chopped
1 lb fresh spinach; stems removed
3/4 teaspoon salt
1/8 teaspoon pepper
1/4 cup peanut butter

Directions
Cook and stir onion and green pepper in oil in 3 quart saucepan until onion is tender. Add tomato and spinach. Cover and simmer until spinach is tender, about 5 minutes. Stir in salt, pepper and peanut butter, heat until hot.

African Vegetable Stew

Ingredients
1 Onion (very large) chopped
1 Swiss chard bunch
1 can Garbanzo beans (known also as chick-peas)
1/2 cup raisins
1/2 cup rice, raw
2 Yams
Several fresh tomatoes (or large can)
1 garlic clove
Salt and pepper, to taste
Tabasco sauce, to taste

Directions
Fry onion, garlic and white stems of chard until barely limp. Add chopped greens and fry a bit. Either peel the yams or scrub them well with a vegetable brush, then slice them into thick slices. Add garbanzos, raisins, yams, tomatoes, salt and pepper. Cook a couple of minutes. Make a well in the center of the mixture in the pot. Put the rice in the well and pat it down until it's wet. Cover and cook until rice is done, about 25 minutes. Add Tabasco sauce to taste.

Benne Cakes

Benne cakes are a food from West Africa. Benne means sesame seeds. The sesame seeds are eaten for good luck. This treat is still eaten in some parts of the American South.

Ingredients
1 cup finely packed brown sugar
1/4 cup butter or margarine, softened
1 egg; beaten
1/2 teaspoon vanilla extract
1 teaspoon freshly squeezed lemon juice
1/2 cup all-purpose flour
1/2 teaspoon baking powder
1/4 teaspoon salt
1 cup toasted sesame seeds

Directions
Preheat the oven to 325F. Lightly oil a cookie sheet. Mix together the brown sugar and butter, and beat until they are creamy. Stir in the egg, vanilla extract, and lemon juice. Add flour, baking powder, salt, and sesame seeds. Drop by rounded teaspoons onto the cookie sheet 2 inches apart. Bake for 15 minutes or until the edges are browned. Enjoy!

Black-Eyed Peas with Ham

Ingredients
3 1/2 cup fresh black-eyed peas or Frozen, thawed
3 cup chicken stock or canned low-salt broth
4 oz. Ham, finely chopped
1 small yellow onion, chopped
2 tablespoon Balsamic vinegar or red wine vinegar
3 large garlic cloves, minced
1 Bay leaf
1/2 teaspoon dried thyme, crumbled
1/4 teaspoon dried crushed red pepper

Directions
Bring all ingredients to boil in heavy large saucepan. Reduce heat and simmer until peas are tender, stirring occasionally, about 45 minutes. Season to taste with salt and pepper.

Papa's Macaroni and Cheese

Ingredients
1 lb. elbow macaroni
1 stick butter
8 oz sharp cheddar cheese
1 can evaporated milk
2 tsp salt
Optional: 1/8 -1/4 lb. small pieces of beef or ham

Directions
Boil 1 lb. elbow macaroni in approximately 2 quarts salted water until just tender but firm. Drain in strainer, rinse with cold water and drain again.

In each casserole, make 2 -3 layers of macaroni, cover each layer with thick slices of butter, and generous slices of sharp cheddar cheese to cover each layer. Add half cup of evap. milk in each casserole before adding the final thick slices of cheese to cover the top.

Bake 50 minutes or until milk is bubbling and cheese is melted and a bit crispy on top.

Makes two 7-inch wide x 3-4 inch deep casseroles. Serves 4-5 people each casserole.

Southern Fried Okra

Ingredients
1 lb Fresh okra cut 1 inch pieces
1 lg Green tomato, diced
1 med Onion chopped
1 Clove garlic, minced (optional)
1 Jalapeno pepper halved & sliced, seeds optional
2 Eggs beaten
1/4 tsp Salt
1/4 tsp Black pepper
1/2 c Milk
1 c Cornmeal
1/4 c Vegetable oil

Directions
Combine okra, tomato, onion, garlic & jalapeno in large bowl. In separate bowl combine eggs, salt, pepper, milk. Pour egg mix over veggies and toss to thoroughly coat. Gradually add cornmeal until mixture on the okra and at the bottom of the bowl soaked up. Continue to toss till ingredients evenly mixed. Mixture will have a gooey consistency.

Heat oil in 10 inch skillet over med. heat until hot. Oil is ready when dash of cornmeal sizzles. Spoon mixture evenly in skillet. Reduce heat to med low. Cover and fry till underside golden brown, 10-15 minutes. Then invert on plate and slide other side up into skillet and cook uncovered 5-8 min until golden brown. Remove from skillet to paper towels to drain excess oil. Serve hot.
Yield: 6 servings

Poems for Kwanzaa

Umoja

Oh Mother Africa
sacred womb of birth
source
of life
shield of protection

Oh Mother Africa
sacred Mother
beauty of all creation

Mother of blessed bounties
bestowed brilliantly
beckoning, beaming brightly
bonds of reverence, freedom, and respect.

Sacred mother, eternal woman
we unite in One Mind
One Divine Spirit
End of male dominance

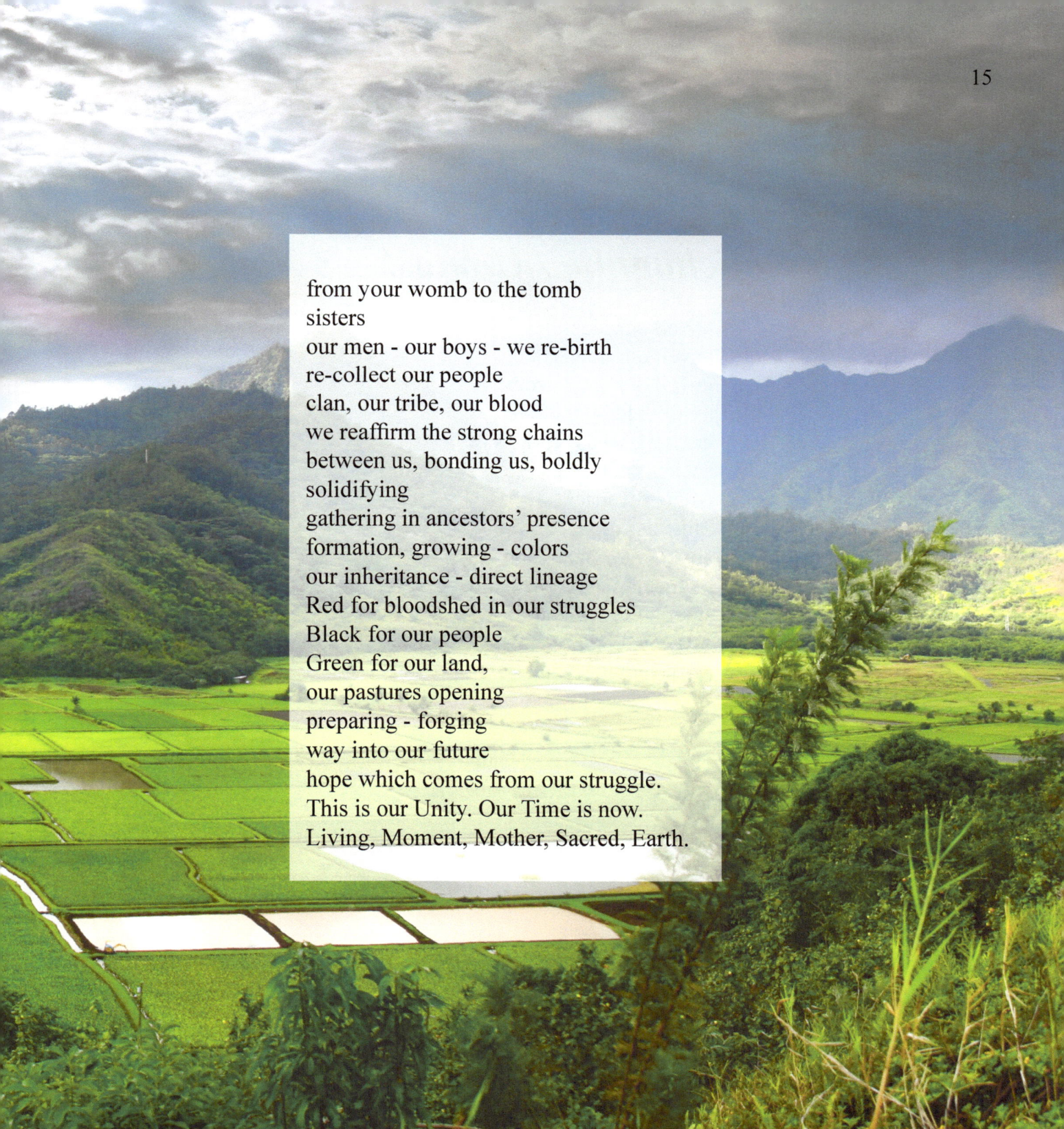

from your womb to the tomb
sisters
our men - our boys - we re-birth
re-collect our people
clan, our tribe, our blood
we reaffirm the strong chains
between us, bonding us, boldly
solidifying
gathering in ancestors' presence
formation, growing - colors
our inheritance - direct lineage
Red for bloodshed in our struggles
Black for our people
Green for our land,
our pastures opening
preparing - forging
way into our future
hope which comes from our struggle.
This is our Unity. Our Time is now.
Living, Moment, Mother, Sacred, Earth.

Kujichagulia / Unmask Us Now

unveil our identity
unveil our power
unveil our quiet truths
murmured by the rivers
crossing sands…grains of
ancient times - ancestors - freedom fighters
women-warriors
Time has come to reveal
unveil our richness on black faces
pigmentations bleached
an afterglow in our eyes
Who owes a forced debt?
by the color of our skin
stolen assets from the motherland
from the Sub-Saharan Africa
oh yes! We smile, we humbly smile
but we say no to 'massah',
we say no to lynching
We say: Unmask us now!

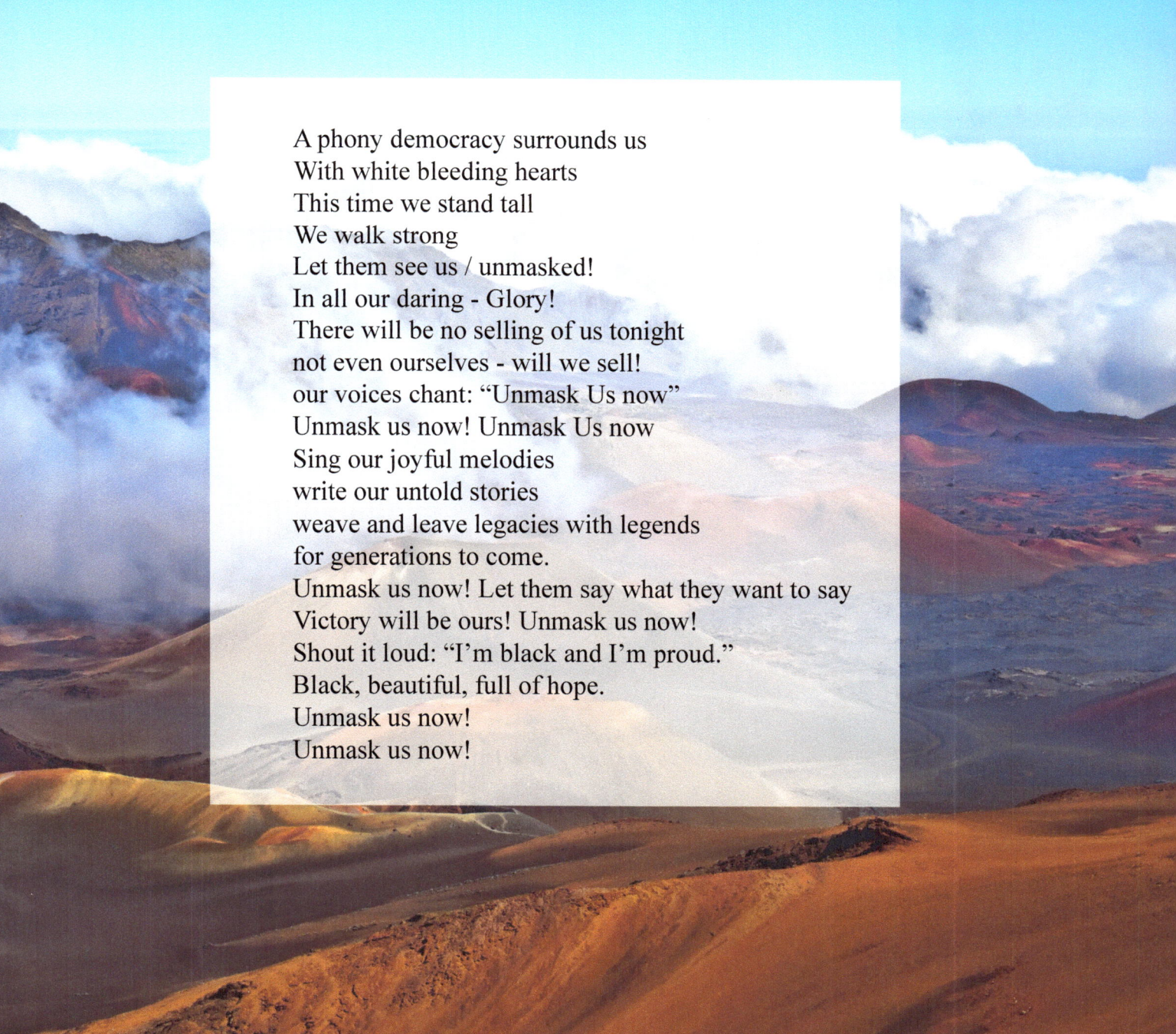

A phony democracy surrounds us
With white bleeding hearts
This time we stand tall
We walk strong
Let them see us / unmasked!
In all our daring - Glory!
There will be no selling of us tonight
not even ourselves - will we sell!
our voices chant: "Unmask Us now"
Unmask us now! Unmask Us now
Sing our joyful melodies
write our untold stories
weave and leave legacies with legends
for generations to come.
Unmask us now! Let them say what they want to say
Victory will be ours! Unmask us now!
Shout it loud: "I'm black and I'm proud."
Black, beautiful, full of hope.
Unmask us now!
Unmask us now!

Ujima / I Lit a Candle For you Today

I lit a candle for you today
No matter how far you run
You take yourself with yourself
Wherever you go
Please choose to grow
I lit a candle for you today

On the backs of our ancestors
Through the strength of Holy songs
Collective Consciousness calls to you.
Community are we

Black like me,
Mother Maui took you into her womb
gentle healing nourishes
love cleanses your wounds
I lit a candle for you today

I lit a candle for you
For the resurrection of your hopes
- dashed -
Purification of your pain
- burned sage -
Wise one

I tried to help
Help tame you
Help calm you
Your fears - tears
Unending questions
Like your place as a Black man
In Hawai`i

I caught the torment in your eyes
Hidden where your fire used to blaze
And burn bright
I lit a candle for you today
To encourage your soul
To return home
Return home
Find peace at last
Black man, find peace.
Awake Thou that sleepest
And let your light shine.
I lit a candle for you today.

Ujamaa / Heritage (Hawai`i)

Hawai`i to me
is Africa you see
a yellow star
nearly perfect from afar
the oceans midst
the black, the white,
the red sand beaches
pristine waterfalls
that lay and wait
as a sacred altar
a traditional Heiau
miles to jog or run
Brown bronzed men
Honey copper ebony women
Hawai`i you see
Is Africa to me
Let us lay where sacrifices are offered
By the blessings of bubbling sounds
Beautiful birds arrived on the backs of
Wind, waves, and wings of other endemic species
Home of the Iwa, `Io, the Nene
Bless the loon, the black heron and the little white
Egrets. Hawai`i you see if Africa to me. Drums throb
In air, feet joyously dance without care, from the beat
Of the Djembe', Ipu, Pahu
Chant: Dink, dinka dinka, dinka, dink,
      Dink, dinka, dinka, dinka, dink
Hawai`i you see is Africa to me.

Nia

From the heartbeat of sacred drums
From the birthplace of humanity
From the cradle of decadence
Percussions echo
One dance
One life
Ultimate results
Drums tonal frequencies
Yield, restoring traditions
Drums call forth a quickening
A call to home
A call to the people
Develop community, restore order
From a thievery existence
Ravaged from the bowels of earth mother
Let us return by way of the sounds
Of our mother's heart beat
Calling her children, restoring her children
Come brothers, come sisters, let us make
Our collective vocation let us rebuild
What will never again be destroyed
And in a new era
We will live forever. There is power
In the beauty of the Blackness of our people
In the hospitality of our homes,
Lies within our hearts.

Kuumba / My Link to Mother

I taste Africa like I taste you
from a distance
love based on an urge
to belong
to connect
with the flowing rivers of
birth
to reconnect,
with the grains of sand
with time
quickly blowing them away again
begin anew
there is a spiritual link
absent of the reality of being there
or a memory of having been there
deep within the walls of soul
there is a longing
a dream

virtual realities of pictures
stored in the chambers of my heart
abundant creativity of music and dance
motherland, my motherland
a mother's continent
treasured with such immense variety of landscape
of freedom, wilderness and wildebeests
who graze on the grassy plains of Namibia.
The Kalahari Desert Bushmen and nomads traditions,
mentality, spirituality, no duality, languages,
vibrations, emanations, sounds, rhythm…
I think of Miriam 'Mama Africa' Makeba
and I feel the vibes and energy - radiating -
grounding me deep within higher ground
a search for identity, one's own identity
is to grow as a person and that growth makes
one stronger. Me, a strong black woman in
Hawai`i, in America.

Imani Is

Imani is the fabric which weaves
the other 6 principles of Nguzo Saba together:

Imani is faith
    in our dignity and humanity;
Imani is continuity
    in our past, present, future;
Imani is unity
    cooperation, collectivity, community;
Imani is love
    family, parents, friends, children;
Imani is not violence.

Imani is dreams
    beauty, belief, creativity;
Imani is creative
    art, aim, aesthetics;
Imani is healing
    medicine, gardens, seeds and harvest;
Imani is intellectual
    problem solving, mathematics, inventions;
Imani is bonding
    business, building, mutual aid;
Imani is not destruction.

Imani is nature
      seasons, elements, growth;
Imani is instinctive
      survival, self-defense, both;
Imani is planting
      honor, respect, humility;
Imani is prayer
      spiritual richness, righteousness;
Imani is not hate.

Imani is work
      building a home, harmony, neighborhoods;
Imani is providing
      for self and those we love;
Imani is protection
      of our fruits for the future;
Imani is not genocide.
Imani serves a need
Imani is a righteous seed
Imani is necessary to success
Imani helps us to rescue and reconstruct
our very lives
Imani keeps us all going
Imani is survival
Imani is victory!

Imani is...
It assumes a future.

Community Photos

Dr. Ayin M. Adams

Dr. Kathryn Waddell Takara

Terri Rainey

George Rainey and Corey Lee

Dr. Ayin M. Adams reading a poem for Kwanzaa

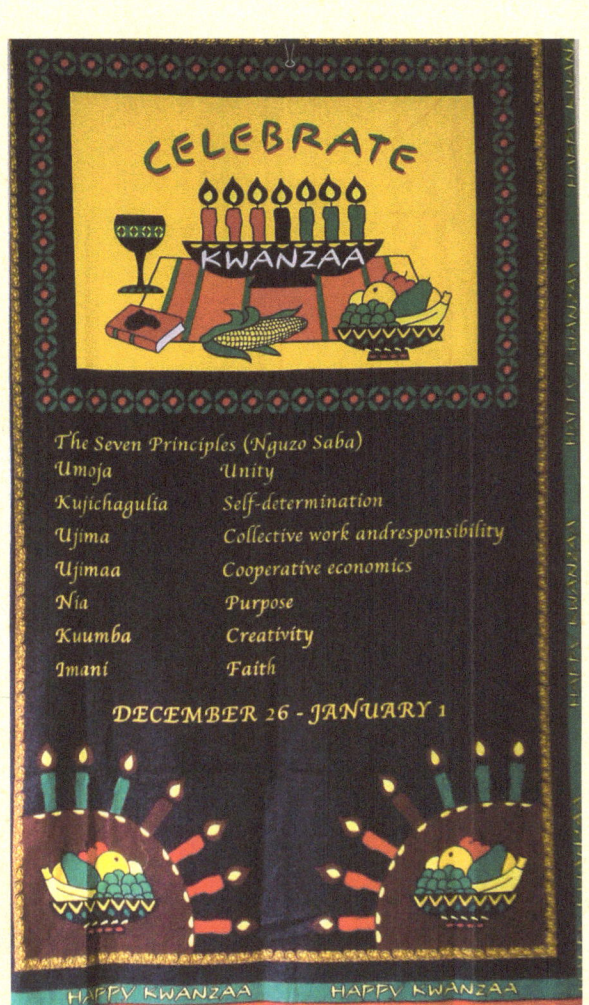

Kwanzaa Cloth with Nguzo Saba
(The Seven Principles)

Location of Photos

Oneloa Beach Pathway at sunset, Maui Hawai`i	Page 12-13
Taro Fields in Kauai Hawai`i	Page 14-15
Haleakala Volcano and Crater in Maui, Hawai`i	Page 16-17
Beach Silhouettes at Sunset	Page 18-19
Iao Needle in Iao Valley State Park, Maui, Hawai`i	Page 20-21
Beautiful Waterfall in Kauai, Hawai`i	Page 22-23
Oahu, Hawai`i Coast	Page 24-25
Silhouette Photo of Dr. Ayin M. Adams	Page 26

Additional Credits

Papa's Macaroni and Cheese	Dr. Kathryn Waddell Takara	Page 11
Imani Is	Dr. Kathryn Waddell Takara	Page 24-25

www.ingramcontent.com/pod-product-compliance
Lightning Source LLC
Chambersburg PA
CBHW060823090426
42738CB00002B/87